HABITAT THRESHOLD

Previously Published Work

Poetry Books:

from unincorporated territory [lukao] (Omnidawn, 2017)
from unincorporated territory [guma'] (Omnidawn, 2014)
from unincorporated territory [saina] (Omnidawn, 2010)
from unincorporated territory [hacha] (Tinfish, 2008 & Omnidawn, 2017)

Co-Edited Anthologies

Geopoetics in Practice (Routledge, 2019)
Indigenous Literatures from Micronesia (U of Hawai'i Press, 2019)
Effigies III: Indigenous Pacific Poetry (Salt Publishing, 2019)
Home Islands: New Writing from Guahan and Hawai'i (Ala Press, 2017)
Chamoru Childhood (Achiote Press, 2008)

HABITAT THRESHOLD

CRAIG SANTOS PEREZ

OMNIDAWN PUBLISHING
OAKLAND, CALIFORNA
2020

Cover photograph by Craig Santos Perez. Picture of the author's father and
daughter at the beach (Oʻahu, Hawaiʻi), 2015.

Poetry-graphs composed in collaboration with Donovan Kuhio Colleps.

Cover typeface: Adobe Garamond Pro
Interior typeface: Adobe Garamond Pro

Cover & interior design by Cassandra Smith

Printed in the United States
by Books International, Dulles, Virginia
On 55# Glatfelter B19 Antique
Acid Free Archival Quality Recycled Paper

Library of Congress Cataloging-in-Publication Data

Names: Santos Perez, Craig, author.
Title: Habitat threshold / Craig Santos Perez.
Description: 1st. | Oakland, California : Omnidawn Publishing, 2020.
Identifiers: LCCN 2019048433 | ISBN 9781632430809 (trade paperback)
Subjects: LCGFT: Poetry.
Classification: LCC PS3619.A598 H33 2020 | DDC 811/.6--dc23
LC record available at https://lccn.loc.gov/2019048433

Published by Omnidawn Publishing, Oakland, California
www.omnidawn.com (510) 237-5472   (800) 792-4957
10 9 8 7 6 5 4 3 2 1
ISBN: 978-1-63243-080-9

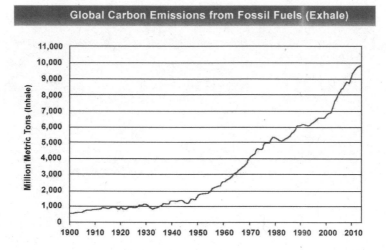

Global Carbon Emissions from Fossil Fuels (Exhale)

Web of Contents

Staying with the trouble requires learning to be truly present, not as a vanishing pivot between awful or edenic pasts and apocalyptic or salvific futures, but as mortal critters entwined in myriad unfinished configurations of places, times, matters, meanings.

—Donna J. Haraway
Staying with the Trouble: Making Kin in the Chthulucene (2016)

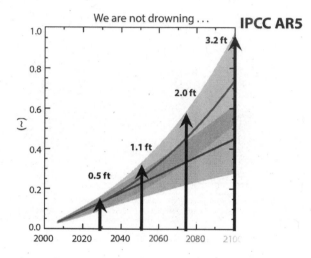

We are not drowning . . .   **IPCC AR5**

3.2 ft

2.0 ft

1.1 ft

0.5 ft

Age of Plastic

The doctor presses the **plastic** probe
against my pregnant wife's belly.
Plastic leaches estrogenic and toxic chemicals.
Ultrasound waves pulse between **plastic**,
tissue, fluid, and bone until the embryo
echoes. *Plastic makes this possible.* My wife
labors at home in an inflatable **plastic** tub.
Plastic disrupts hormonal and endocrine systems.
After delivery, she stores her placenta
in a **plastic** freezer bag. *Plastic is the perfect
creation because it never dies.* Our daughter
sucks on a **plastic** pacifier. *Whales,
plankton, shrimp, and birds confuse **plastic**
for food.* The **plastic** pump whirrs;
breastmilk drips into a **plastic** bottle.
Plastic keeps food, water, and medicine fresh—
yet how empty **plastic** must feel
to be birthed, used, then disposed
by us: degrading creators. *In the oceans,
one ton of **plastic** exists for every three tons
of fish*—how free **plastic** must feel
when it finally arrives to the paradise
of the Pacific gyre. *Will **plastic** make
life impossible?* Our daughter falls
asleep in a **plastic** crib, and I dream
that she's composed of **plastic**,
so that she, too, will survive
our wasteful hands.

"Plastic is
wholly
swallowed up
in the fact
of being
used:
ultimately,
objects
will be invented
for the sole
pleasure
of using them.
The hierarchy
of substances
is abolished:
a single one
replaces
them all:
the whole world
can be
plasticized,
and even
life itself…"

—Roland Barthes,
Mythologies (1957)

Halloween in the Anthropocene *(a necropastoral)*

Darkness spills across the sky like an oil plume.
The moon reflects bleached coral. Tonight, let us
praise the sacrificed. Praise the souls of black
boys, enslaved by supply chains, who haul bags
of cacao under west African heat. "Trick or treat,
smell my feet, give me something good to eat,"
sings a girl dressed as a Disney princess.
Tonight, let us praise the souls of brown girls
who sew our clothes as fire unthreads sweatshops
into charred flesh. "Trick or treat, smell my feet,
give me something good," whisper kids disguised
as ninjas. Tonight, let us praise the souls of Asian
teens who manufacture toys and tech until gravity
sharpens their bodies enough to cut through suicide
nets. "Trick or treat, smell my feet, give me," chant
kids masquerading as cowboys and Indians. Tonight,
let us praise the souls of native youth, whose eyes
are open-pit uranium mines, veins are poisoned
rivers, hearts are tar sands tailings ponds. Tonight,
let us praise our mothers of fallout, mothers of cancer
clusters, mothers of slow violence, *pray for us*, because
our costumes won't hide the true cost of our greed.
Tonight, let us praise our mothers of extinction,
mothers of miscarriage, mothers of cheap nature,
pray for us, because even tomorrow will be haunted…

Teething Borders[1]

Our daughter won't stop crying,
so we massage her red, swollen gums
with our fingers and sing: "Row, row, row
your boat, gently down the stream,
merrily, merrily, merrily, merrily, life is
but a dream." On the news,
a makeshift boat filled with refugees
capsized in the Mediterranean.
Those with life jackets float
like bright yellow teeth. The others:
swallowed by the sea's territorial mouth.
How many fled Boko Haram, the vanishing
of Lake Chad, the floods in East Africa?
How many more will be desiccated
by the Sahara desert, or macerated by
traffickers at Libya's salivating shore?
How many will survive only to be
gnawed by the jaws of Europe?
Our daughter won't stop crying,
so we give her a teething ring
to chew. "Row, row, row your boat,
gently down the stream, merrily,
merrily, merrily, merrily, life is…"

---

[1] "Borders are set up to define the places that are safe and unsafe, to distinguish us from them. A border is a dividing line, a narrow strip along a steep edge. A borderland is a vague and undetermined place created by the emotional residue of an unnatural boundary. It is in a constant state of transition. The prohibited and forbidden are its inhabitants."
—Gloria Anzaldúa, Borderlands/La Frontera: The New Mestiza (1987)

On the news, refugees from
Central and South America are detained
at the US/Mexico border and separated from
their children—some are so young they still
have baby teeth. Others: unaccompanied.
How many fled drug cartels, abusive
men, and gang violence? How many
more will be devoured by La Bestia,
dehydrated by the Sonoran desert,
and torn apart by La Migra's incisors?
How many will survive only to be spit out
from the rotting cavities of America?
Our daughter won't stop crying,
so we give her a cold bottle to nurse.
"Row, row, row your boat, gently
down the stream…" More than half
of all border walls around the world
have been built since 2001—"justified"
by wars on terror. But refugees are
not the true terror. The true terror is
that 34,000 people are forced from
their homes every day, and by the end
of this year, 65 million will be uprooted,
and in the coming years, climate change
will displace millions more—half will be
children. We swaddle our daughter
in our arms. "Row, row, row…"
A "caravan" of migrants approaches
our teething borders. Will we build
a tender country, where the only
documents needed for citizenship
are dreams of sanctuary?

Disaster Haiku

after cyclone winston after typhoon yutu after hurricane maria after…

the world
briefly sees us
only *after*
the eye
of a storm
sees us

Rings of Fire

Honolulu, Hawai'i

We host our daughter's first birthday party
during the hottest April in history.

Outside, my dad grills meat over charcoal;
inside, my mom steams rice and roasts

vegetables. They've traveled from California,
where drought carves trees into tinder—"*Paradise*

is burning." When our daughter's first fever spiked,
the doctor said, "It's a sign she's fighting infection."

Bloodshed surges with global temperatures,
which know no borders. "If her fever doesn't break,"

the doctor continued, "take her to the Emergency
Room." Airstrikes detonate hospitals

in Yemen, Iraq, Afghanistan, South Sudan…
"When she crowned," my wife said, "it felt like rings

of fire." Volcanoes erupt along Pacific fault lines;
sweltering heatwaves scorch Australia;

forests in Indonesia are razed for palm oil plantations—
their ashes flock, like ghost birds, to our distant

rib cages. Still, I crave an unfiltered cigarette,
even though I quit years ago, and my breath

no longer smells like my grandpa's overflowing ashtray—
his parched cough still punctures the black lungs

of cancer and denial. "If she struggles to breathe,"
the doctor advised, "give her an asthma inhaler."

But tonight we sing, "Happy Birthday," and blow
out the candles together. Smoke trembles

as if we all exhaled
the same flammable wish.

Thirteen Ways of Looking at a Glacier
recycling Wallace Stevens

XIII

Among starving polar bears,
the only moving thing
was the edge of a glacier.

XII

We are of one ecology
like a planet
in which there were once 200,000 glaciers.

XI

The glacier absorbs greenhouse gas.
We are a large part of the biosphere.

X

Humans and animals
are kin.
Humans and animals and glaciers
are kin.

IX

We do not know which to fear more,
the terror of change
or the terror of uncertainty,

the glacier calving
or just after.

VIII

Icebergs fill the vast ocean
with titanic wrecks.
The mass of the glacier
disappears, to and fro.
The threat
hidden in the crevasse
an irreversible clause.

VII

O vulnerable humans,
why do you engineer sea walls?
Do you not see how the glacier
already floods the streets
of the cities around you?

VI

I know king tides,
and lurid, unprecedented storms;
but I know, too,
that the glacier is involved
in what I know.

V

When the glacial terminus broke,

it marked the beginning
of one of many waves.

IV

At the rumble of a glacier
losing its equilibrium,
every tourist in the new Arctic
chased ice quickly.

III

Shell explored the poles
for offshore drilling.
Once, we blocked them,
in that we understood
the risk of an oil spill
to a glacier.

II

The sea is rising.
The glacier must be retreating.

I

It was summer all winter.
It was melting
and it was going to melt.
The last glacier fits
in our warm hands.

A Sonnet at the Edge of the Reef
the Waikīkī Aquarium

We dip our hands into the outdoor reef exhibit
and touch sea cucumber and red urchin
as butterflyfish swim by. A docent explains:
once a year, after the full moon, when tides swell
to a certain height, and saltwater reaches the perfect
temperature, only then will the ocean cue coral
polyps to spawn, in synchrony, a galaxy of gametes,
which dances to the surface, fertilizes, opens,
forms larvae, roots to seafloor, and grows, generation
upon generation. At home, we read a children's
book, *The Great Barrier Reef,* to our daughter
snuggling between us in bed. We don't mention
corals bleaching, reared in labs, or frozen.
And isn't our silence, too, a kind of shelter?

Rainbow After the Massacre
Mānoa Valley District Park

We watch kids play baseball and soccer ::

             this is a "normal" Sunday ::

hours earlier :: fifty people were murdered

      at a night club in Orlando, Florida :: the killer

armed with a legal assault rifle :: this is a "normal" day

      in America ::

a country where being lesbian, gay, bi, trans, or two-spirit

      is deemed "abnormal" :: where gun control

is "abnormal" :: without warning :: gray clouds empty

"To write in the queer::eco::poetics realm

      is to begin by interrogating the construction

of what is *natural*, and all of what *natural* implies

      (inevitable, innate, normal, nonhuman, pristine, etc.)."

             —Tamiko Beyer "Notes towards a queer::eco::poetics" (2010)

rounds of rain :: we run for shelter

in a country where everything "normal" polices

our families, bodies, desires, and futures ::

yet all we want is to hold our friends ::

feel their pulse ::

say *thank you* :: for being :: for teaching us that "queer"

is not "against nature" but nature itself dancing

beyond borders :: singing beyond difference :: loving

beyond hate :: thank you for teaching us

how to transform fear into pride :: how to translate

a kiss

into the erotic language of hope ::

the sun returns ::

a rainbow arcs across the valley ::

may it touch :: everywhere :: into music ::

Care
for World Refugee Day

Our daughter wakes from her nap and cries.
I pick her up, press her against my chest,

and whisper: "Daddy's here, daddy's here."
Here is the island of Oʻahu, 8,500 miles from Syria.

But what if Pacific trade winds suddenly
became flames and shrapnel indiscriminately

barreling towards us? What if shadows cast
upon our windows aren't plumeria tree branches,

but soldiers and terrorists marching?
"Daddy's here, daddy's here," I whisper.

Would we reach the Mediterranean in time?
Am I strong enough to straighten my legs

into a mast, balanced with the pull and drift
of the currents? Am I brave enough to bear her

across the razor wires of foreign countries
and racial hatred? Could I plead: "please,

help us, please, just let us pass, please,
we aren't suicide bombs." Could I keep

walking if my feet crack like Halaby pepper fields
after five years of drought, after this drought

of humanity? "Daddy's here, daddy's here."
Trains and buses rock back and forth,

back and forth, back and forth, to detention
centers. But what if our desperate boat

      capsizes?

Could I inflate my body into a buoy
to hold her above rough waves?

"Daddy's here, daddy's…"
Will drowning be the last lullaby

of the sea?
Or will we carry

      each *other*
      towards the horizon

                        of care?

Love in a Time of Climate Change
recycling Pablo Neruda's "Sonnet XVII".

I don't love you as if you were rare earth metals,
conflict diamonds, or reserves of crude oil that cause
war. I love you as one loves the most vulnerable
species: urgently, between the habitat and its loss.

I love you as one loves the last seed saved
within a vault, gestating the heritage of our roots,
and thanks to your body, the taste that ripens
from its fruit still lives sweetly on my tongue.

I love you without knowing how or when this world
will end. I love you organically, without pesticides.
I love you like this because we'll only survive

in the nitrogen rich compost of our embrace,
so close that your emissions of carbon are mine,
so close that your sea rises with my heat.

Chanting the Waters

for the Standing Rock Sioux Tribe and water protectors around the world

"water moves the deep shift of life
back to birth and before…"

—Linda Hogan, "The Turtle Watchers" (2008)

Say: "Water is _____ !"
    because our bodies are 60 percent water—
        because my wife labored for 24 hours
    through contracting waves—
because water breaks forth from shifting tectonic plates—
      Say: "Water is _____ !"
    because amniotic fluid is 90 percent water—
        because she breathed and breathed and breathed—
        because our lungs are 80 percent water—
because our daughter crowned like a new island—
     Say: "Water is _____ !"
    because we tell creation stories about water—
       because our language flows from water—
because our words are islands writ on water—
because it takes more than three gallons of water
     to make a single sheet of paper—
      Say: "Water is _____ !"
    because water is the next oil—
because 180,000 miles of U.S. oil pipelines leak everyday—
because we wage war over gods and water and oil—

Say: "Water is _____ !"

because our planet is 70 percent water—

because only 3 percent of global water is freshwater—

because it takes two gallons of water
to refine one gallon of gasoline—

because it takes 22 gallons of water
to make a pound of plastic—

because it takes 660 gallons of water
to make one hamburger—

because it takes 3,000 gallons to make one smart phone—

because the American water footprint is 2,000 gallons a day—

Say: "Water is _____ !"

because a billion people lack access to drinking water—

because women and children walk 4 miles every day
to gather clean water and deliver it home

Say: "Water is _____ !"

because our bones are 30 percent water—

because if you lose 5 percent of your body's water
you become feverish—

because if you lose 10 percent of your body's water
you become immobile—

because our bodies won't survive a week without water

Say: "Water is _____ !"

because corporations privatize, dam, and bottle our waters–

because plantations divert our waters—

because animal slaughterhouses consume our waters—

because pesticides, chemicals, lead, and waste
poison our waters

Say: "Water is _____ !"

because they bring their bulldozers and drills and drones—

because we bring our feathers and lei and sage and shells
and canoes and hashtags and totems—

because they call us savage and primitive and riot—

because we bring our treaties
        and the Declaration on the Rights of Indigenous Peoples—
                    because they bring their banks and politicians
and dogs and paychecks and pepper spray and bullets—
                    because we bring our songs and schools and prayers
                            and chants and ceremonies—
            because we say stop! keep the oil in the ground—
    because they say shut up! and vanish—
                because we are not moving—
        because they bring their police and private militia—
because we bring all our relations
        and all our generations and all our livestreams—
                        Say: "Water is ____ !"
                because our drumming sounds like rain after drought
                            echoing against taut skin—
                because our skin is 60 percent water—
        Say: "Water is ____ !"
    because every year millions of children die
from waterborne diseases—
        because every day thousands of children die
                        from water-borne diseases—
            because, by the end of this poem,
five children will die from water-borne diseases—
                    Say: "Water is ____ !"
                because our daughter loves playing in the ocean—
            because someday she'll ask, "where does the ocean end?"—
        because we'll point to the dilating horizon—
    Say: "Water is ____ !"
                because our eyes are 95 percent water—
                    because we'll tell her ocean has no end—
            because sky and clouds lift ocean—
        because mountains embrace ocean into blessings of rain—
because ocean-sky-rain fills aquifers and lakes—

because ocean-sky-rain-lake flows into the Missouri River—
because ocean-sky-rain-lake-river returns
to the Pacific and connects us
to our cousins at Standing Rock—
because our blood is 90 percent water—
Say: "Water is _____ !"
because our hearts are 75 percent water—
because I'll teach our daughter my people's word for water:
"hanom, hanom, hanom"—
so the sound of water
will always carry her home—
Say: "Water is _____ !"
"Water is _____ !"
"Water is _____ !"

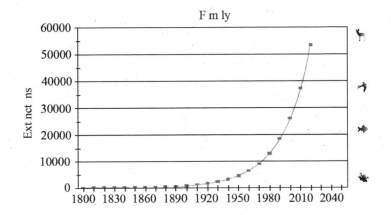

(Silent) Spring Haiku

dead
   bees
 seed
the
  bed

       of
     our
      garden
          what
      flow
    -ers

  un-
  pol-
   lin-
    at-
   ed
  ?

"Everywhere was a shadow of death."
—Rachel Carson, Silent Spring (1962)

Blood Ivory
Honolulu Zoo, for World Elephants Day

When we reach the elephant enclosure,
I lift our daughter up so she can see them
playing in shallow ponds. "Look," I say.
"They love the water, just like you."
Today, 96 elephants are being massacred
across Africa's scarred savannah.
Armed poachers surround the herds,
who stomp, trumpet, and encircle
their calves. Bullets, those small human

tusks, bite through thick, wrinkled skin.
Do the men still feel awe or majesty,
or do they only feel their own awful
poverty as they sever the incisors,
once used to split bark and forage?
Warlords will sell this "white gold"

to be carved into jewelry, relics, and art,
then smuggled across the planet,
our man-made elephant graveyard.
This year, 35,000 will be slain.
Our daughter waves goodbye to them
as we walk towards the exit. Do we
build zoos to save what we've sacrificed,
to display what we dominate,
or to cage our own wild urge to kill

every breathing being? Our daughter
plays with a stuffed elephant doll
in the gift shop. "Look," I say.
"It has ears, eyes, and a mouth,
just like you." She touches its tusks,
smiles, then touches her own teeth.

The United States is the second largest market for ivory, after China. Hawai‘i is the third largest market within the United States, after New York and California, both of whom passed laws banning the sale of ivory. This poem was written in support of Senate Bill 2647 (2016), a proposed Hawai‘i state law that prohibited selling, offering to sell, purchasing, trading, or bartering ivory, as well as other parts of species that are listed in the Convention on International Trade in Endangered Species, the International Union for Conservation of Nature, and the Endangered Species Act.

One fish, Two fish, Plastics, Dead fish
recycling Dr. Seuss

Some fish are sold for sashimi,
some are sold to canneries,
and some are caught by hungry slaves
to feed what wealthy tourists crave!

Farmed fish, Fish sticks, Frankenfish, Collapse

From the Pacific to the Atlantic,
from the Indian to the Arctic,
from here to there,
dead zones are everywhere!

Overfishing, Purse seine, Ghost fishing, Bycatch

This one has a little radiation.
This one has a little mercury.
O me! O my! What schools
of bloated fish float by!

Here are fish that used to spawn, but now the water is too warm

Some are predators and some are prey,
Who will survive? I can't say.
Say! Look at its tumors! One, two, three…
How many tumors do *you* see?

Two fish, One fish, Filet-o-Fish, No fish

"An m ls surro nded our anc st rs. An m ls wer th ir fo d, cl th s, adv rs ries, c mp nions, jok s, and th ir g ds…In th s age of m ss ext nct n and th ind str al zat on of l fe, it is h rd to touch th sk n of th s l ng and de p c mp n onsh p. N w we surro nd th an m ls and cr wd th m fr m th ir hom s…An mal ty and hum n ty ar one, xpr ss ons of th pl n t's br ll ant inv nt ven ss, and yet th an m ls ar leav ng th wor d and n t ret rn ng."

—Al son H wth rne Dem ng
Zool g es: On An m ls and th Hum n Sp r t (2 14)

Thanksgiving in the Plantationocene

Thank you, instant mashed potatoes, your bland taste
makes me feel like an average American. Thank you,

incarcerated Americans, for filling the labor shortage
and packing potatoes in Idaho. Thank you, canned cranberry

sauce, for your gelatinous curves. Thank you, native tribe
in Wisconsin, your lake is now polluted with phosphate

discharge from nearby cranberry bogs. Thank you, crisp
green beans, you are my excuse for eating dessert

á la mode later. Thank you, indigenous migrant workers,
for picking the beans in Mexico's farm belt, may your bodies

survive the season. Thank you, NAFTA, for making life so cheap.
Thank you, Butterball Turkey, for the word, "butterball,"

which I repeat all day (say it with me): "butterball, butterball,
butterball," because it helps me swallow the bones of genocide.

Thank you, dark meat for being so juicy (no offense, dry
and fragile white meat, you matter too). Thank you, 90 million

factory farmed turkeys, for giving your lives during the holidays.
Thank you, factory farm workers, for clipping turkey toes

and beaks so they don't scratch and peck each other
in overcrowded, dark sheds. Thank you, stunning tank,

for immobilizing most of the turkeys hanging
upside down by crippled legs. Thank you, stainless

steel knives. Thank you, scalding-hot de-feathering tank,
for finally killing the last still conscious turkeys.

Thank you, turkey tails, for feeding Pacific Islanders
all year round. Thank you, empire of slaughter,

for your fatty leftovers. Thank you, tryptophan,
for the promise of an afternoon nap.

Thank you, dear readers, for joining me
at the table of this poem. Please join hands,

bow your heads, and repeat after me:
"Let us bless the hands that harvest and butcher

our food, bless the hands that drive delivery trucks
and stock grocery shelves, bless the hands that cooked

and paid for this meal, bless the hands that bind
our hands and force feed our endless mouth.

May we forgive each other and be forgiven."

This Is Just To Say
recycling William Carlos Williams

I have eaten
the "meats"
that were in
the lab

and which
you were probably
growing
for "burgers"

forgive me
they were impossible™
so heme
and so eco

Cockroach Ode

My oldest memory
is waking from a nap
to a cockroach staring
at me. It doesn't move
as I clutch its dark body
with my toddler fingers.
When I bite down, it hisses
—legs, wings, fluttering.
Have you ever seen
a decapitated cockroach
scurry? Today, rising seas
threaten their populations
because they can't swim.
Don't worry: they breed
a *fuck-you, will-to-thrive,*
there-are-too-many-of-us
attitude. They're the first
terrestrial beings to birth
in space. Pre-Jurassic,
post-nuclear, future-milk.
They've learned to avoid
the violent light of human
eyes. I can still feel
its antennae searching
my tongue for the foul
saliva of extinction.
Blessed be the cockroaches,
for they shall inherit
the warming earth.

We Aren't the Only Species

who age who change who language who pain who play who pray who
save who mate who native who take who break who invade who claim
who taste who want who talk who crawl who walk who yawn who trauma
who laugh who care who hear who fear who steal who heal who friend
who remember who sex who nest who settle who smell who help who eat
who feed who greed who sleep who see who need who belong who bleed
who speak who breathe who breathe who breathe who think who drink
who sing who thirst who birth who kill who smile who lick who listen
who kiss who give who sick who piss who shit who swim who migrate
who die who fight who cry who hide who sign who mourn who mourn
who mourn who work who school who tool who colonize who bond who
protect who hope who lose who love who lonely who touch who moan
who drown who hurt who hunt who run who hunger who nurse who
suffer who build who trust who bury who future who house who house
who house on this our only

Echolocation
for "J35, Tahlequah"

My wife plays
with our daughter
while I cook dinner.
On the news,
we watch
you struggle
to balance
dead calf on
your rostrum.

Days pass.
We drive
our daughter
to preschool and
to the hospital
for vaccinations.
You carry your
child's decom-
posing body
a thousand
nautical miles
until every wave
is an elegy,
until our planet
is an open
casket.

How do you say,
"sorry," in your
dialect of sonar,
calls, and whistles?

What is mourning
but our shared
echolocation?

Today, you let go
so her body
could fall and
feed others.
Somehow,
you keep
swimming.
We walk
to the beach
so our daughter
can build
sandcastles.
May she grow
in the wake
of your resilience.
May we always
remember:

love is our wildest
oceanic instinct.

Endangered Haiku

sea

    turtle

      hatch

        -lings

            crawl

             across

               this

                 page

                 into

                         pre-

                           carious

                             waves

The Last Safe Habitat

for the Kauaiʻi ʻŌʻō, whose song was last heard in 1987

I don't want our daughter to know
that Hawaiʻi is *the bird extinction capital
of the world*. I don't want her to walk
around the island feeling haunted
by tree roots buried under concrete.
I don't want her to fear the invasive
predators who slither, pounce,
bite, swallow, disease, and multiply.
I don't want her to see paintings
and photographs of birds she'll never
witness in the wild. I don't want her to
imagine their bones in dark museum
drawers. I don't want her to hear
their voice recordings on the internet.
I don't want her to memorize and recite
the names of 77 lost species and subspecies.
I don't want her to draw a timeline
with the years each was "first collected"
and "last sighted." I don't want her to learn
about the Kauaʻi ʻŌʻō, who was observed
atop a flowering ʻŌhiʻa tree, calling
for a mate, day after day, season after
season, because he didn't know he was
the last of his kind—

       until one day, he disappeared,
forever, into a nest of avian silence.
I don't want our daughter to calculate
how many miles of fencing is needed
to protect the endangered birds

that remain. I don't want her to realize
the most serious causes of extinction
can't be fenced out. I want to convince her
that extinction is not the end. I want
to convince her that extinction is
just a migration to the last safe habitat
on earth. I want to convince her
that our winged relatives have arrived
safely to their destination: a wondrous
island with a climate we can never
change, and a rainforest fertile
with seeds and song.

"What is lost
when a species,
an evolutionary lineage,
a way of life,
passes from the world?
What does this loss mean
within the particular
multispecies community
in which it occurs:
a community of humans
and nonhumans,
of the living
and the dead?"

—Thom Van Dooren,
Flight Ways: Life and Loss
at the Edge
of Extinction (2014)

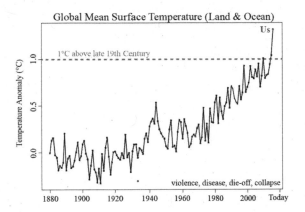

Global Mean Surface Temperature (Land & Ocean)

Christmas in the Capitalocene
recycling Irving Berlin

I'm dreaming of a fake Christmas,
just like the plastic trees made in China,
where factories glisten and workers miss
their distant children and villages.
May your labor protests be organized,
and may all your Christmases be paid.

I'm dreaming of a rich Christmas,
unlike the temp jobs we all know,
where forklifts hiss and scanner guns click
the aisles and shelves of online orders.
May your picking volume targets be met,
and may all your Christmases be peak.

I'm dreaming of a black Christmas,
just like the boys we used to know,
where cops fire munitions and citizens petition
in the malls and streets of White America.
May your murderers be indicted,
and may all your Christmases be just.

I'm dreaming of a warm Christmas,
just like the ones we'll all soon know,
where floods have risen and cities riven
by extreme storms and tornadoes.
May our Arctic ice sheets be frozen,
and may all our Christmases be safe.

Postcards from Taiwan

Yvonne, a graduate student who wrote her thesis on Native American eco-criticism, picks me up in a hybrid Prius from the Kaoshiung airport. On the sidewalks, adults walk to work and children walk to school wearing breathing masks. Is the smog here made in China? A man sits cross-legged, meditating, amidst the crowd. What is the sound of 1,000 mopeds revving?

Monkeys line the road to the multi-species National Sun Yat-Sen University. The faculty and graduate students I meet study the environmental humanities. I read my eco-poetry to them and discuss Pacific literature, sacred islands, and environmental justice. They ask about Trump, who called the president of Taiwan a few days before I arrived. I bow my head in shame.

The next day, Yvonne drives us to the Taiwanese Indigenous Cultural Center. Our English language guide wears a Baltimore Orioles jersey, made in China. Tourists wear masks and cough during the show. After, we go to the museum. The museum tour guide wears a mask with the insignia: "Polar Bear." He alternates between talking and coughing.

During lunch, Yvonne orders us beer made in Taiwan. It tastes universal. Then we drive further up the mountain and stop to eat cold Taiwanese jelly. It tastes local. We drive even further up the mountain until we arrive at the village of Wutai. Elementary school kids weave baskets on an open-air American basketball court. There's a colorful mural that tells a harvest story. "There used to be a river flowing through the mountains," Yvonne says. "Before the dam." The riverbed is the color of concrete.

Yvonne suggests I sleep during the long drive back to the city. Two hours later, the sound of a 1,000 mopeds wakes me. We enter the underground parking garage of an 85-story skyscraper in Kaoshiung. We take the elevator to a fancy buffet restaurant on the 39th floor. Hsinya, the professor who sponsored my visit and co-editor of *Aspects of Transnational and Indigenous Cultures*, joins us for dinner. I fill my plate with fresh local fish and roast beef imported from Australia. I thank Hsinya for publishing my poem, "Thirteen Ways of Looking at a Glacier," in the *Newsletter of the Comparative Literature Association of the Republic of China*. I joke that a Pacific Islander poem about the Arctic appearing in a Chinese literary journal is either a "climate anomaly" or "the new normal."

In the morning, Yvonne drives me to the airport. The meditating man has either gone to work or he has transcended the quotidian. I wish I could transcend the long check-in line for my flight. While waiting, I don a breathing mask in order to fit in. I grow accustomed to wearing the mask; it feels like my own private quarantine. As the plane takes off towards the turbulent horizon, I start to feel nauseous. I hope there's a doctor on board. And by "doctor," I don't mean someone with a Ph.D. in the environmental humanities.

Hours later, we begin our bumpy, alt-right descent into America. At the airport, I follow the crowd towards "Global Entry." "Take off your mask and look at the camera," the white customs officer commands. I wonder: can the software facially recognize my disgust with the American electorate? He grabs my passport, like Trump grabs pussy, and stamps it with the salute of a new era. I claim my baggage, discard my mask, and cough. I have something dangerous to declare.

The Flatulencene

car (ex-   haust) hu-   man   (bu   -rp)

sh-   ale   (fr-   ack)

gr-   een   -house (g-   as) bo- vine   corp

-us (o   -pen) por   -ous   sm- og

ass -embl   -age (me   -thane)

ru- men   (em -it)   stom-

aches (mou -th) a-   nal

(sph-   inc -ter)

to   -ilet   sew -er

fer-   men   -ted   (wi -nd)

gr- ass   cow   (bac-   teria)

"inti   -mate   str-   angers"

(tab- oo)   err-   ant leak -age

vol- canic   (e-   rupt   -ion

(sul- phur) si-   lent bu -tt dead-   ly

America

recycling Allen Ginsberg

America you've stolen everything and now I have nothing.
America $1.3 trillion in student loan debt, 2016.
I can't stand my climate anxiety.
America when will you end your wars of terror?
Go fuck yourself with your 7,000 nuclear warheads.
I haven't had my fair trade coffee yet don't bother me.
America when will you pay reparations for slavery?
When will you be worthy of 5 million indigenous people?
America why are your libraries full of the houseless?
When will you feed your hungry children?
I'm sick of your obscene inequality.
When can I go to the supermarket and buy what I need with my
      good poems?

America you and I will never be a perfect union.
Your enhanced propaganda and interrogation techniques
      are too much for me.
You make me want to Wikileak.
There must be some way to end your settler colonialism.
America I refuse to give up my high-speed internet.
America stop surveilling me I'm doing something private.
I've been reading the newspapers for months, every day a cop is
      not indicted for murder.
America I refused to enlist in the Army after high school
      and I'm not sorry.
Your military is the largest carbon emitter on the planet.
Don't deny it: war fuels global warming.
America Is your environmental strategy, "scorched earth"?
I vote to legalize marijuana every chance I get.

Then I sit in my house for days on end and Netflix binge.
My mind's made up there's going to be an online petition!
America when will you pass the Green New Deal?
You should've seen me reading *The End of Nature*.
My yoga teacher thinks my chakras are almost perfectly aligned.
America I won't stand for your Star Spangled Banner.
I have indigenous visions and anarchist vibrations.

America I'm hashtagging you.
America are you going to let your intellectual life be run by Fox
      News? Its white talking heads are always talking about
      what matters. All lives matter. Blue lives matter.
      Everybody matters but me.
It occurs to me that I'm not America. I'm taking bad selfies again.

Sea levels are rising against me. I haven't got a polar bear's chance.
I'd better consider my adaptation plan. My adaptation plan consists of
moving to Blockadia with two cases of SPAM, a kombucha mother, and a
hand-sewn journal of unpublished solarpunk poems that go 100 miles on
a full battery, community orchards of prosody, and millions of heirloom
words that grow in metaphoric gardens of renewable joy across blank
pages. America, I have abolished carbon emissions; ICE, prisons, Wall
Street, Walmart, the US-Mexico border wall, private property, Congress,
the electoral college, Amazon, the military industrial complex, Monsanto,
and capitalism are the next to go. My ambition is to be President despite
being born on Guam.

America how can I write an inaugural poem in your fascist mood?
I will continue, like Elon Musk, my poems are as ambitious as
      his automobiles more so they're actually affordable.
America I'm selling loosie political poems for $1 apiece on your
      bloody sidewalks don't shoot!

America free Leonard Peltier!
America Mumia Abu-Jamal must not die!
America grow food not lawns!
America we are Trayvon Martin!
America drop poems not bombs!
America give me fully-automated eco-luxury communism or give
          me death!

America when I moved to Hawaiʻi my wife took me to a
          Hawaiian sovereignty event they fed us local poi and
          luau stew and sweet potatoes for free and the speeches
          were inspiring and the hula dancers were angelic and the
          chanters breathed their once endangered language back
          to life and the sincere poets made me cry and no one will
          ever forget how you overthrew the Hawaiian Kingdom
          in 1893 because our struggle will remain creative and non-
          violent. All of us there were rainbow warriors.

America you were never great.
Are you fake news?
America this is the impression I get after feeding from Trump's
          Twitter trough.
America I don't want to be a drone operator and murder civilians at
          weddings.
I'm nearsighted and a hopeless romantic anyway.
America I'm putting my native shoulder to the medicine wheel.

Earth (Day) Haiku
Honolulu, Hawaiʻi

white

hippies   sprout

from

yoga
mats

&

dance   naked

to claim   the commons

This Changes Everything

We attend the first Hawai'i screening of Naomi Klein's documentary at the mall movie theatre. The line for the documentary is long, almost as long as the Hawai'i endangered species list. Unlike the endangered species list, there aren't many natives in this line.

The theatre feels small and uncomfortably full, like an overbooked ark. The white people around us start coughing, which triggers intergenerational trauma in my body. Our daughter starts to become restless, too, so my wife breastfeeds her until she falls asleep. I nurse my organic, raw Kombucha to calm my nerves and improve my gut microbiome.

I, too, have always kind of hated films about climate change. Not because they feature cliche polar bears, but because they're all made by cliche white people. In the climate movement, indigenous peoples are the new polar bears. We sport a vulnerable-yet-charismatic-species-vibe, an endangered-yet-resilient-chic, a survive-and-thrive-swagger. Plus, we cry "native tears," which are the most affective tears.

Do you remember "The Crying Indian" PSA from the Keep America Beautiful campaign, which launched on Earth Day in 1971? A non-native actor, "Iron Eyes Cody," plays a Native American who rows his canoe down a littered river and past smoking factories, until he lands on a dirty beach that leads to a busy highway. A voice says, "Some people have a deep abiding respect for the natural beauty that was once this country. And some people don't. People start pollution, people can stop it." It ends with a closeup on his "native tears."

When the natives in "This Changes Everything" cry, the white people in the theatre cry "white tears" extra-loudly. I hate it when white people cry extra-loudly, as if they've never seen native people cry in real life. When the documentary shows polluted native lands, the white people gasp extra-loudly. I hate it when white people gasp extra-loudly. "Stop gasping so loudly!" I shout in my head. "Everything already changed for native peoples centuries ago!"

We sneak out of the theatre during the post-documentary discussion. I whisper to my wife: "The Geological Society should refer to this era of human destruction as the *Wypipocene*." She says we should make a documentary about how climate change is finally making white people uncomfortable. Titled: "Melting Glaciers, White Tears."

Hush, Little Planet
a geo-engineering lullaby

Hush, little planet, don't say a word,
Daddy's gonna buy you an air filter,
And if greenhouse gas won't go away,
Daddy's gonna buy you aerosol spray,
And if the atmosphere won't cool,
Daddy's gonna buy you rocket fuel,
And if colonizing Mars don't succeed,
Daddy's gonna buy you sulfate seeds,
And if reflective clouds disappear,
Daddy's gonna buy you space mirrors,
And if mirrors don't deflect the sun,
Daddy's gonna buy you mineral dust,
And if that dust don't heal the ocean,
Daddy's gonna buy you a floating island,
And if this man-made island drowns,
You'll still be the sweetest planet around.

New Year's Eve and Day in the Chthulucene

December 31

I take a bubble bath, alone. On my smartphone, the Pandora app plays "Under Pressure," "Purple Rain," and "Faith." I weep at the crossroads of celebrity death, social media, and late-late-capitalism. I open the Facebook app to like something in this world. Friends post pictures of black eyed peas, noodles, grapes, pomegranates, roast pork, cooked greens, lentils, and cake. I like their posts for good luck and universal basic income. Then I share a meme that juxtaposes a picture of a feast somewhere with a picture of impoverished children eating bread crumbs somewhere else. No one likes it.

I click the link, "This is the official poem of 2016," and read a trending poem about a parent/realtor trying to sell the "good bones" of a broken-down house/the world to her children/potential buyers. I'm interrupted when I hear my daughter crying in the other room. In most eco-literature, children represent the vulnerable, hopeful future. Yet children in real life represent the tantrum of the present. I think about thousands of her dirty diapers that will take 450 years to decompose—outliving us all.

I get dressed and join my family in the living room. As midnight nears, we blow bubbles. Our daughter doesn't poke them; instead, she kisses each bubble so they pop on her lips. It's sooo cute that I forget the cheap champagne, the predictable countdown, the ball dropping, the global detonations.

January 1

Fuck sunrise hikes. I resolve to sleep in. When I wake, I open my
Facebook app and share a meme that juxtaposes a picture of fireworks
somewhere with a picture of war somewhere else. No one likes it.

So I brew fair trade coffee, argue with myself about drinking milk, and
read Timothy Morton's *The Ecological Thought* (2010). He argues that
"ecology isn't just about global warming, recycling, and solar power—
and also not just to do with everyday relationships between humans and
nonhumans. It has to do with love, loss, despair, and compassion. It
has to do with depression and psychosis. It has to do with amazement,
open-mindedness, and wonder. It has to do with doubt, confusion, and
skepticism. It has to do with concepts of space and time. It has to do
with delight, beauty, ugliness, disgust, irony, and pain. It has to do with
consciousness and awareness. It has to do with ideology and critique.
It has to do with reading and writing. It has to do with race, class, and
gender. It has to do with sexuality. It has to do with ideas of self and the
weird paradoxes of subjectivity. It has to do with society. It has to do with
coexistence."

Bored, I turn on the television. During the American football game, two
activists rappel from the stadium rafters and unfurl a banner: "US Bank:
DIVEST #NoDAPL." At no point is the game interrupted. At no point
is my body exercised or dieted. At no point is my life detoxed or plastic
free. At no point is my internet addiction controlled or meaningful social
relations nurtured. At no point is climate change combatted.

Fuck sunset hikes. Fuck the new year's known knowns. Fuck the new
year's known unknowns. Fuck the new year's unknown unknowns. I
resolve to eat countless chicken wings, write chicken-less recipes for the

kitchens of the future, and binge watch climate change documentaries and zombie movies on Netflix until I fall asleep.

In my dream, an Uber driver named Cthulhu Oddkin, picks me up at the crossroads of technophilia, precarity, and the sharing economy. We drive away from the slums and empty skyscrapers of the neoliberal megacity, past the rusted factories, past the GMO plantations, past the data server farms, past the oil refineries, past the private prisons, and past the deep sea port. Along the way, we discuss scientific, social, and philosophical reforms, foreign journeys, distant shores, buffoonish travelers, perplexing customs, harmonious societies, sovereign crypto-currencies, etc.

Hours later, we arrive at a native reserve named, "Utopia." We stop along the poisoned river and its pipeline. I get out and ask the water: "Is the apocalypse coming?" A one-eyed salmon floats to the surface and says: "Your apocalypse began centuries ago. And it's accelerating." I return to the car, but Cthulhu has disappeared. An AI voice states: "We all have unequal, uncertain futures."

Good Fossil Fuels

recycling Maggie Smith

Earth is ruined, though I deny this to my children.
Earth is ruined, and I've ruined it
in a thousand carbon-intensive ways,
a thousand carbon-intensive ways
I'll share with my children. The planet is at least
fifty percent polluted, and that's a conservative
estimate, though I deny this to my children.
For every sea there is waste thrown into the sea.
For every sacred place, a place fracked, logged,
bombed into dust. Earth is ruined and the planet
is at least half polluted, and for every green
garden, there's a toxin that would poison you,
though I deny this to my children. I am trying
to sell them doubt. Any decent capitalist,
profiting from a climate disaster, squeals on about
good fossil fuels: This growth could be sustainable,
right? We could make this growth sustainable.

Nuclear Family

7

In the beginning, _____ and _____
stood on the bridge of heaven and stirred the sea
with a jeweled spear until the first island was born.
Then one day, men who claimed to be gods
said: "Let there be atomic light," and there was
a blinding flash, a mushroom cloud, and radiating
fire. "This will end all wars," they said.
"This will bring peace to the divided world."

6

In the beginning, _____ and _____
ascended from the First World of darkness
until they reached the glittering waters
of this Fourth World, where the yellow snake,
_____ , dwelled underground.
Then one day, men who claimed to be gods
said: "Let there be uranium," and they dug
a thousand unventilated mines. They unleashed
_____ and said: "This will enrich us all."

5

In the beginning, _____ spoke the islands
into being and created four gods to protect
each direction. The first people emerged
from a wound in _____'s body.
Then one day, men who claimed to be gods

said: "Let there be thermonuclear light,"
and there were countless detonations. "Bravo!"
They exclaimed, "This is for the good of mankind."

4

In the beginning, _____ transformed
the eyes of _____ into the sun and moon,
and his back into an island. Then her body
transformed into stone and birthed my people.
Then one day, men who claimed to be gods
said: "Let there be a bone seeker," and trade winds
rained strontium 90 upon us, and irradiated ships
were washed in our waters. And they said:
"This is for national security."

3

In the beginning, _____ created earth from mud.
Then his younger brother, _____ , carried
a woven basket full of the first people to the Great Basin.
Then one day, the men who claimed to be gods
said: "Let there be plowshare," and the desert
cratered, and white dust snowed upon the four corners.
And they said: "This is for peaceful construction."

2

"The militarization of light has been widely acknowledged as a
historical rupture that brought into being a continuous Nuclear Age,
but less understood is the way in which our bodies are written by these

wars of light." —Elizabeth DeLoughrey, "Radiation Ecologies and the Wars of Light" (2009)

1

In the beginning, there was no contamination.
Then the men who claimed to be gods said:
"Let there be fallout," and our lands and waters
became proving grounds, waste dumps,
and tailings. "Let there be fallout," and there was
a chain reaction of leukemia, lymphoma,
miscarriages, birth defects, and cancer.
"Let there be fallout," and there's no half-life of
grief when a loved one dies from radiation disease,
there's no half-life of sorrow when our children
inherit this toxic legacy, this generational
and genetic aftermath, this fission of worlds.

0

Let there be the disarmament of the violent nucleus
within nations. Let there be a proliferation of justice
and peace across our atomic cartographies: from
Hiroshima and Nagasaki to the Marshall Islands.
From the Navajo and Shoshone Nations to Mororua,
Fangataufa, In Ekker, Kirimati, Maralinga, Amchitka,
Malan, Montebello Islands, Malden Island, Pokhran,
Ras Koh Hills, Chagai District, Semipalatinsk,
Novaya Zemlya, Three Mile Island, Chernobyl,
Punggye-ri, and Fukushima. Let there be peace
and justice for the downwinders, from Utah
to Guam to every irradiated species.

Praise Song for Oceania
for World Oceans Day

"…as if there is a path where beings truly meet,
as if I am rounding the human corners."

—Linda Hogan, "The Turtle Watchers" (2008)

~

praise your capacity for birth
 fluid currents and trenchant darkness
 praise our briny beginning
 source of every breath

~

praise your capacity for renewal
 ascent into clouds and descent into rain
 praise your underground aquifers
 rivers and lakes, ice sheets and glaciers
 praise your watersheds and hydrologic cycles

~

praise your capacity to endure
 the violation of those who map you aqua nullius
 who claim dominion over you
 who pillage and divide your body
 into latitudes and longitudes
 who scar your middle passages

praise your capacity to survive
      our trawling boats breaching
            your open wounds and taking
                  from your collapsing

                                        depths

praise your capacity to dilute
      our heavy metals and greenhouse gases
            sewage and radioactive waste
                  pollutants and plastics

praise your capacity to bury
      our shipwrecks and ruined cities
            praise your watery grave
                  human reef of bones

praise your capacity to remember
      your library of drowned stories
            museum of lost treasures
                  your vast archive of desire

praise your tidalectics
        your migrant routes
                and submarine roots

praise your capacity to smother
        whales and fish and wash them ashore
                to save them from our cruelty
                        to show us what we're no longer allowed to take
                to starve us like your corals starved and bleached
        liquid lungs choked of oxygen

praise your capacity to forgive

please forgive our territorial hands and acidic breath
        please forgive our nuclear arms and naval bodies
                please forgive our concrete dams and cabling veins

please forgive our deafening sonar and lustful tourisms
        please forgive our invasive drilling and deep sea mining
                please forgive our extractions and trespasses

praise your capacity for mercy

please let my grandpa catch just one more fish

        please make it stop raining soon
             please make it rain soon

please spare our fragile farms and fruit trees
       please spare our low-lying islands and atolls
          please spare our coastal villages and cities
             please let us cross safely to a land without war

praise your capacity for healing
       praise your cleansing rituals
          praise your holy baptisms

please protect our daughter
       when she swims in your currents

praise your halcyon nests
    praise your pacific stillness
        praise your breathless calm

praise your capacity for hope

praise your rainbow warrior and peace boat
          praise your hokule'a and sea shepherd
                    praise your arctic sunrise and freedom flotillas

praise your nuclear free and independent pacific movement
         praise your marine stewardship councils and sustainable fisheries

                    praise your radical seafarers and native navigators

praise your sacred water walkers
         praise your activist kayaks and traditional canoes
              praise your ocean conservancies and surfrider foundations

praise your aquanauts and hyrdolabs
         praise your Ocean Cleanup and Google Oceans
              praise your whale hunting and shark finning bans

praise your sanctuaries and no take zones
         praise your pharmacopeia of new antibiotics
              praise your #oceanoptimism and Ocean Elders
                    praise your wave and tidal energy
                        praise your blue humanities

praise your capacity for echolocation
   praise our names for you that translate
     into creation stories and song maps
       tasi : kai : tai : moana nui : vasa :
         tahi : lik : wai tui : wonsolwara

praise your capacity for communion

praise our common heritage
   praise our pathway and promise to each other
     praise our most powerful metaphor
       praise your vision of belonging

praise our endless saga
   praise your blue planet
     one world ocean

praise our trans-oceanic
   past present future flowing
     through our blood

Acknowledgments

This book is dedicated to my children, wife, parents, siblings, and extended family and friends.

Thanks to my editor, Rusty, for your continued guidance and belief in my work. Thanks to Omnidawn for your support of my poetry over the years. Thanks to Cassie for her beautiful design of the cover and interior.

Thanks to the following journals and anthologies for publishing earlier versions of these poems: Poetry Magazine, The New Republic, Tin House, Rattle, Grist, Ghost Fishing: An Eco-Justice Poetry Anthology, Big Energy Poets: Ecopoetry Thinks Climate Change, Planet in Peril (WWF/The Climate Coalition), The EcoTheo Review, About Place Journal, Asian American Writers Workshop The Margins: Transpacific Literary Project on "Plastic," The Southeast Review, Carbon Copy, Atlantic Studies, The Brooklyn Rail, Civil Beat Hawaiʻi, Poetry Daily, The Hawaiʻi Review, COG Journal, NACLA: Report on the Americas, Yellow Medicine Review, The Tiny Magazine, Rascal Literary Journal, Dispatches, Waxwing Literary Journal, Ghost Town, Under a Warm Green Linden, Apogee Journal, Poets Reading the News: Journalism in Verse, Nomadic Ground Coffee literary inserts, Public Pool, Summit Magazine, Extinction Witness, Bulletin of the World Meteorological Organization (Switzerland), Newsletter of the Comparative Literature Association (China), Guangming Daily Newspaper (China), Voice and Verse Poetry Magazine (Hong Kong), Norwegian Writers Climate Campaign (Norway), Tazmania Quaker Newsletter (Australia), Rabbit: Nonfiction Poetry (Australia), Plumwood Mountain (Australia), Train Literary Journal (Canada), Arc Poetry Magazine (Canada), Across Currents: Connections Between Atlantic and (Trans)Pacific Studies (England), and the BBC World Service: Cultural Frontline ("Art in the Anthropocene") (England).

Thanks to the organizers of the following events, in which many of these poems were first performed: The International Union of the Conservation of Nature:

World Conservation Congress; The Sydney Environment Institute Lecture Series (Australia); the Hawai'i Conservation Alliance Conference; The International Conference on Environmental Futures; the Smithsonian Asian Pacific American Center 'Ae Kai: A Culture Lab on Convergence of Time, Space, Nature, and Us; the Symposium on Art in Hawai'i; the SENCER Summer Institute on Water; the Archipelagoes, Oceans, and the Americas conference (Australia), the Festival of Pacific Arts (Guam), and the Native American Indigenous Studies Association Conference.

Thanks to the following scholars and poets for inspiring some of the lines in "Praise Song for Oceania": Epeli Hau'ofa, Derek Walcott, Elizabeth DeLoughrey, Rob Wilson, Astrida Neimanis, Peter Neill, Sylvia Earle, Édouard Glissant, and Albert Wendt.

Thanks to Hawaiian filmmaker, Justyn Ah Chong, for making "Praise Song for Oceania" into a short film. Thanks to the organizers of the following festivals, conferences, and events at which the poem-film was screened: the Guam International Film Festival (2017), the Hawaii International Film Festival (2017), the Native Spirit Film Festival (United Kingdom, 2017), the Transoceanic Visual Exchange (Australia & Barbados, 2017), the Los Angeles Asian Pacific Film Festival (2018), The Earth Day Film Festival (2018), the Wairoa Maori Film Festival (New Zealand, 2018), the Pasifika Film Festival (Australia, 2018), the Philadelphia Asian American Film Festival (2018), the Maoriland Film Festival (New Zealand, 2019), and the Elements International Environmental Film Festival (Vancouver, 2019). The film also screened at the Hita I Hanom: We are Water Exhibition of the Guam Humanities Council (2016), the UNESCO Ocean Literacy for All Conference (Italy, 2017), the Sustaining our Seas conference (Australia, 2017), COMCAST Cinema Asian America (2018), and in Hawaiian Airline In-Flight Programming (2018). "Praise Song for Oceania" was featured on the United Nations World Oceans Day online portal, sponsored by the Intergovernmental Oceanographic Commission. The poem-film won a 2018 Silver Lei Award for Short Film Competition of the Honolulu Film Awards.

Cover Photograph Credits

Top Image: "Monacobreen Glacier Calving, Svalbard, Arctic." Photographer: Gary Bembridge. This image was originally posted to Flickr by "garybembridge" at https://flickr.com/photos/ 8327374@N02/ 20277016232. It was reviewed on 4 August 2015 by Flickreview and was confirmed to be licensed under the terms of the Creative Commons Attribution 2.0 Generic license (https://commons. wikimedia.org/wiki/File:Monacobreen_Glacier_Calving,_Svalbard,_Arctic_ (20277016232).jpg#filelinks).

Middle Image: Taken by author. Photograph of author's father and daughter on a beach in Oʻahu, Hawaiʻi, 2015.

Bottom Image: "A Helicopter Drops Water on the Wildfire in California." Photographer: Andrea Booher/FEMA. Description: "Helicopters drop water and fire retardant on the Harris fire, near the Mexican border, to stop the wildfire from advancing. Currently the fires in Southern California have burned nearly 350,000 acres." San Diego, CA, October 25, 2007. Public Domain (https:// commons.wikimedia.org/wiki/File:FEMA_-_33364_-_A_helicopter_drops_ water_on_the_wildfire_in_California.jpg).

Back Cover Image: "Microplastics." Source: NOAA Marine Debris Program. Description: "When exposed to light, plastics break down into small pieces through a process known as 'photodegradation.' These small bits of plastic, known as microplastics, make up the majority of items found in the so-called 'Pacific Garbage Patch,' where they float suspended in the water column. For more information about marine debris and how it can be prevented, visit the NOAA Marine Debris Program website." This image was originally posted to Flickr by NOAA Marine Debris Program at https://flickr.com/ photos/78725676@N06/7656713582. It was reviewed on 21 January 2018 by Flickreview and was confirmed to be licensed under the terms of the Creative Commons Attribution 2.0 Generic license (https://commons.wikimedia.org/ wiki/File:Microplastics_(7656713582).jpg).

AUTHOR BIOGRAPHY

Dr. Craig Santos Perez is an indigenous Chamorro from the Pacific
Island of Guåhan (Guam). He is the author of four collections of poetry,
the co-editor of five anthologies, and the co-founder of Ala Press, an
independent publisher dedicated to Pacific Islander literature.

He earned an MFA in Creative Writing from the University of San
Francisco and a Ph.D. in Comparative Ethnic Studies from the University
of California, Berkeley. He is an associate professor in the English
department, and an affiliate faculty with the Center for Pacific Islands
Studies and the Indigenous Politics Program, at the University of Hawai'i,
Mānoa. He teaches creative writing, Pacific literature, and eco-poetry.

Craig serves on the editorial boards of Sun Tracks, an indigenous literature
series with the University of Arizona Press, and The Contemporary
Pacific, an academic journal of Pacific Islands Studies. He is the series
editor for the New Oceania Literary Series with the University of
Hawai'i Press. He also serves on the Board of the non-profits, Pacific
Writers Connection and Pacific Islanders in Communication. He is a
participating scholar for the Humanities for the Environment Asia-Pacific
Observatory. He has also served as faculty for Kundiman and VONA.

He has received the Pen Center USA/Poetry Society of America Literary
Prize, American Book Award, Hawai'i Literary Arts Council Award,
Lannan Foundation Literary Fellowship, Ford Foundation Fellowship,
and University of Hawai'i Chancellors' Citation for Meritorious Teaching.
He has been a finalist for the Los Angeles Times Book Prize and the
Kingsley Tufts Award.

Habitat Threshold
by Craig Santos Perez

Cover photograph by Craig Santos Perez. Picture of the author's father and
daughter at the beach (Oʻahu, Hawaiʻi), 2015.

Cover typeface: Adobe Garamond Pro
Interior typeface: Adobe Garamond Pro

Cover & interior design by Cassandra Smith

Printed in the United States
by Books International, Dulles, Virginia
On 55# Glatfelter B19 Antique
Acid Free Archival Quality Recycled Paper

Publication of this book was made possible in part by gifts from
Katherine & John Gravendyk in honor of Hillary Gravendyk,
Francesca Bell, Mary Mackey, and The New Place Fund

Omnidawn Publishing
Oakland, California
Staff and Volunteers, Spring 2020

Rusty Morrison & Ken Keegan, senior editors & co-publishers
Kayla Ellenbecker, production editor
Gillian Olivia Blythe Hamel, senior editor & book designer
Trisha Peck, senior editor & book designer
Rob Hendricks, marketing assistant & *Omniverse* editor
Cassandra Smith, poetry editor & book designer
Sharon Zetter, poetry editor & book designer
Liza Flum, poetry editor
Matthew Bowie, poetry editor
Juliana Paslay, fiction editor
Gail Aronson, fiction editor
Izabella Santana, fiction editor & marketing assistant
SD Sumner, copyeditor